Living a Legendary Life

LWS
BOOKS
©2006
www.lwsbooks.com

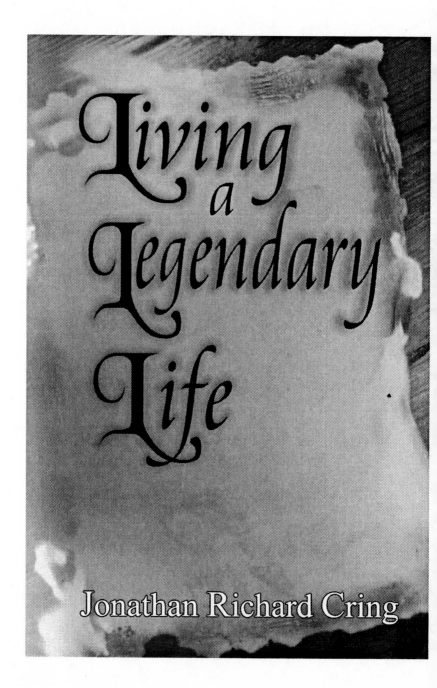

Living a Legendary Life

Jonathan Richard Cring

LWS Books
P.O. Box 833
Hendersonville, TN 37077-0833
(800) 643-4718 ext. 74
lwsbooks.com

LWS Books are available at special quantity discounts for
bulk purchases for sales promotions, premiums, fund-
raising, and educational needs. Special books or book
excerpts also can be created to fit specific needs.
For details, write: LWS Books Special Markets,
P.O. Box 833, Hendersonville, TN 37077

ISBN 10: 1-59975-622-6
ISBN 13: 978-1-59975-622-6

Library of Congress Control Number: 2006900003

For information on the authors touring schedule visit:
WWW.JANETHAN.COM

Cover Design by Angela Cring, Clazzy Studios

Manufactured and Printed in the United States

Table of Contents

Sittings

-INTRODUCTION-

Everybody gets fifteen minutes of fame.

Seemingly a clever, harmless phrase. At worst, promoting cynicism and at best, encouraging the masses to aspire to greatness.

Perhaps there is nothing wrong with buying ten lottery tickets a week, hoping to become the new millionaire. It could be just fine to sign up with Publisher's Clearinghouse Sweepstakes, dreaming of the knock on the door. Maybe it's all right to clip coupons, squirreling away your savings for that trip around the world.

After all, isn't this just part of the American dream—every boy and girl can grow up to be either President of the United States or wealthy, feathering their nest with abundance?

What's the harm?

Consider—while pursuing the dream, it is very easy to lose the value of the waking hours. While stashing money and seeking fame, moments pass where what we already possess is underrated and the power in our life is untapped.

It is a farce; I mean that everybody gets fifteen minutes of fame.

Most human beings will remain in obscurity, not known by more than two or three thousand people throughout their lifespan.

This is the truth.

There is an old saying that the truth will make you free. But free to do what? Or perhaps, free to be what? It is a freedom from lies trapping us in false goals, leading down paths to nowhere.

After all, what is so horrible about obscurity? What is so wrong with being loved by a few people instead of hearing the screaming adulation of the faceless masses?

Someone needs to sit down and tell every man, woman and child, "Hey! You're not going to be famous! But you can be legendary."

For after all, there are many people throughout history who gained fame, but left nothing of quality behind—no meaningful legacy.

A legendary life.

A decision to take our life and stay alert and practical—as if it were the only life we will ever have.

For after all, it is.

-Sitting One-
Seen in Secret

It really doesn't make any difference to me what name you use. Perhaps someday, when we cross over the vast chasm of misinformation, we will discover that there is an actual name above all other names.

But for the sake of discussion in this book, please understand I don't really care what name or title you use.

What I'm talking about is the name we prefer for that Unseen Beyond Us That Sees All.

Call him God, Allah, Jesus, Vishnu, Mohammed, Jehovah, Enlightened One or even Larry. It makes no difference to me.

Even agnosticism and atheism receive no condemnation from this author.

Yet, in the practical application of our everyday lives, and for the sake of pursuing the excellence of a legendary existence, it seems to me, we must acknowledge an Unseen That Sees All—even if this personage is of our own creation.

So if you will allow me in this book, I will call this Unseen, Larry—the generic deity.

My main problem with organized religion is that it worships a god who shows up for praise and worship and then disappears, leaving us, in the rest of our week, to our own devices. The end result? Some of the greatest agnostics in the world are the truly avid followers occupying mosque, church, synagogue and monastery. They have a form of godliness but deny the real power and message of a lifestyle—that being: *we believe, so we can receive, becoming more generous in ourselves and more open to others.* This should be the conclusion of a religious encounter, or spirituality, rather than being a cure for what ails humankind, becomes actually the disease infesting us.

So for the sake of this sitting, please allow me to call this unseen presence, Larry. I think it will prevent any disgruntled religious folk from feeling I expressed favoritism and to those not so inclined to theological matters, it will introduce a friendly, neutral presence

Larry is of us.

Larry knows how we work. He knows our drawbacks.

Our greatest weakness?

Theory over substance.

We just prefer discussion to decision. We relish committees to commitment and favor argument to agreement.

And why is this?

Because laziness is our mooching second cousin and fussiness our adopted Jewish mother.

So, mulling over principle robs all the time for principled action. Political maneuvering eliminates policy change.

Larry knows our weakness.

Maybe it's a creative flaw—a design malfunction. Maybe it's a symptom of general wear and tear. Or, more likely, it's deterioration in our consciousness.

We have chosen repeat over repent.

After all, spirituality in theory is interesting. Spirituality in practice is a festering reminder of our inadequacy. So it's much easier to believe that Larry extends grace to us, cutting us slack for our shortcomings and allowing us to muddle on in our lives in some sort of bewildered dream cloud.

But here's the shocker: Larry sees.

Even in the moments when we feel like it doesn't make any difference—those times we think that effort is anal—Larry sees.

It is important to know that we are not alone in our actions. Or, perhaps better phrased, our inactions. Most of the sins of the human race are transgressions in omission instead of commission. In other words, we fail most often by delaying, not by prematurely jumping in.

We have just trained ourselves to be spectators to our own lives, victims of chance and circumstance, adrift on the seas of fate.

Larry disagrees.

The first step to leading a legendary life is realizing that Larry sees, Larry cares and Larry is prepared to reward those souls who dare to become intimately involved in their own lives by making quality choices.

For Larry sees in secret. And once we bring our secret life under our own review, we begin to set in motion true empowerment to garner success. And what is that success? The real success comes from deriving soul satisfaction at the end of a well-thought-out day.

Yes. Larry sees in secret. Not so he can punish, but rather, alert, and therefore, bestow benefit upon those folks who become caretakers of their own space.

But how do we override the sensation that some things just really don't matter?

1. **Slow your life down.** Take the time to enjoy the time to redeem the time to have the time to create the time to make the time mean more.

And this isn't just another "stop and smell the roses" speech. This is slowing down our lives, avoiding the horrendous practice of multi-tasking (which is really just producing the possibility of multi-erroring) and finding out the unexplored value of the common. For instance, the grocery store is not only stocked with food, but with people, surprises, deals, samples and conversation for those shoppers who will slow the pace down a bit and take in the whole experience. The jobsite is not merely the joint where we pick up our paycheck, but rather, a place to rehearse excellence, interact with people who disagree and discover better use of time and energy.

Larry sees—not because he's nosy, but because Larry knows we are better people when we do more than hit our marks but instead, pace ourselves and enjoy the journey.

2. **Notice.** That's right—a single word.

We are a visual people needing a vision.

There are others trying.

Notice.

Every morning, Larry and Nature put together a fireworks extravaganza that we glibly call "dawn." And every night they repeat the process—dusk.

Notice.

Honestly, you're not going to be very good at it at first. You may find it silly. But every explosion of pleasure began with our thinking that it was either silly or gross. Take sex, for instance. At twelve years of age, each of us would have sworn that we would never be involved in such shenanigans. It sounded nasty. We swore to avoid it at all costs.

We were wrong.

We're also wrong to stop ourselves from pursuing the *knack of notice* that leads to revelation.

Remember: All blessing is encased by inconvenience.

Notice one thing today that you did not notice yesterday. Then you'll have three hundred sixty-five things in your bank of discovery at the end of the year—not to mention the interest you have earned from other folks around you.

3. **Acknowledge.** You do understand, there are people who are trying to be

involved with others by being more attentive to their own life.

Acknowledge when you see them already doing what you want to do.

Acknowledge courtesy.

Acknowledge excellence.

Acknowledge tenderness.

Acknowledge awareness.

Acknowledge when someone has pursued something further than expected.

There are people who have actually figured out that Larry is watching.

Even though there seems to be a vast *human-wing conspiracy* promoting oblivion, still, the instant we contend that there are no really caring, aware people, someone will crop up in our midst and do something really delightfully human—human in the sense of how we were intended to be.

Surprise!

What is the purpose of possessing the greatest brainpower on the planet and using it to stumble through a series of repetitive chores?

What is the value of having a capacity to love at a fevered intensity and yawn our way through a bunch of boring relationships?

To live a legendary existence means we must live as if we understand that we are seen—even in our secret moments. Larry isn't trying to condemn us, but rather motivate us to become keepers of our own destiny.

Larry is watching because he gives a damn and hopes that we can learn to feel the same way.

-Sitting Two-
You Never Get What You Need

It takes a lot to make New York City rise up in horror and surprise—a town filled with a sophisticated (although some people would insist "jaded") populace. Yet there was one thing for certain that brought disapproval from every borough— aggressive homeless people.

For you see, New York did not mind the tin cups, or even destitute folks lying in doorways. But when the homeless rose from their haunches of neediness and began to accost cars with dirty rags intending to earn some money by cleaning windshields, well, something had to be done.

Spoofs were quickly written by comedy shows, long discussions conducted in parlors and eventually, laws passed to prohibit the ever-present needy from any form of entrepreneurism.

Now don't get me wrong. I'm not trying to say that I want someone running a dirty towel across my windshield, leaving horrific streaks and then demanding payment. I just found it fascinating how disturbed we became when the creatures of the street rose up and tried to make a place for themselves in the glut of activity.

The reason is: *we never get what we need.*

There is something deep within our species that despises neediness. The notion of poverty and neediness, in a sense, frightens us all.

We just don't like needy people.

We may sympathize. We may feel for them. But neediness causes us to want to escape; after all, there is a danger of the plague being contracted.

Yes, the most dastardly part of lack is that it begets lack.

Needy people are eventually surrounded by needy people, the only fellowship being the wail of woe.

You just don't ever get what you need.

Life may threaten to bestow the request, only to jerk it away at the last moment—a fresh wound in the heart of the already disenfranchised.

Why?

"Why" is not so difficult to answer as it may seem.

Whether you view this universe and planet as a creation, or as an evolution, you must understand of a certainty, it is a

20

corporation. That's right. There is business being conducted in the cosmos every day. And because it's a business, it has two goals. Number one, produce and make a profit. Number two, make things run smoothly.

Needy people grind the gears of the corporation of the universe to a halt through their incessant demands and ongoing desires.

Perhaps mercy would be in order in certain cases. Perhaps it would be all right for us to take care of a small percentage of the needy on the planet if it remained tiny. But it doesn't and won't. For after all, why would any of us pursue excellence if our needs could be met through request? We are basically a lazy species who derive our sustenance from using an enterprising mind, free of any sense of neediness. Think about it. Do we really expect our CEO, Larry, to run the assembly line and man the phone in the complaint department? So let's understand how it works: need is resolved in one of two ways. Either some human being comes along and fulfills my lack, or I get off my keister, stop expressing the need and find a way either to live without it or a way to get it.

Revelation: Larry's Corporation has no coffee breaks, and no suggestion box. It works because we do. The CEO seems to be a great benefactor because, like on any job, we don't bother him. The more contact you have with your boss, the less likely you will stay there very long, because people in charge don't normally interact with people who are working unless they are either correcting them or, for a very brief time, patiently listening to their questions.

I think, somewhere along the line, because of sentimentality, we have bought into the concept that the earth is a family (though I seriously doubt that "need" is accepted very well even in a family situation. Uncle Charlie better damn well get a job, if you know what I mean...) The earth is not a family, and I repeat, it is and always will be a living, breathing corporation seeking profit, pursuing improvement and tossing around the idea of excellence.

Need is sand in the gears of progress.

Need is the buzzing fly during a summer's nap.

Need is the pesky ant crawling on the checkerboard tablecloth spread for the picnic of life.

Need is the telemarketer during the dinner hour.

Need is the final story droned out by the boring vacationer following three hours of senseless slides.

Need is what we all embrace and hate simultaneously.

You never get what you need.

I suppose if I were to sum up the message of every religion or philosophy into one word, when all the slabs of stone and all the mildewed pages of books have been reviewed, the one word that would remain is, REPENT. In other words, don't tell me what you need. Tell me that you're ready to change.

Repent makes things work. Yes, love is the oil that smoothes the engine. But love has one great drawback: it does grow weary in well doing.

Repent is the marching orders for an army of lovers. What should we repent of? Neediness.

So, if *we* have need?

Simple enough. Change a need to a want. Because the truth of the matter is, *we do sometimes get what we want.* Want is merely putting a motor on a need. It's having a paddle in your boat, an idea in your head, an agenda for accomplishment, even if it's inadequate to the solution. We admire those souls who try. In the United States, we tend to be very open to those from foreign lands, as long as they make an attempt to be American. But when they stand before us only needy, unable to speak the language or adapt to a common theme and culture, we may slap ourselves for being intolerant, but honestly, we just don't like them.

Because you never get what you need.

But you sometimes get what you want because grace is so much more easily extended to those who are obviously still hanging in the struggle.

How do you change a need to a want?

1. *Never talk about it but feel free to act it out.* If you need to dig a hole in your back yard, don't sit in your living room and lament the lack of a tool. Walk out, get on your knees and begin to dig in the ground with your hands. Someone will see you and there is an increased possibility they will arrive with a shovel to aid you. People like to give to people who are on the way to getting because we like to feel that what we have given has been the salvation rather than a drop in the bucket.

2. *Never use the word "need."* There are certain letters which, when formed together, don't just make words. They create reactions from others. I will make a

suggestion of a few: war, rape, death, nigger, spic, fat-ass, liberal, conservative, pagan, evil, stupid, meaningless, and fool. And these are just a few. These are words that when spoken, pre-determine the profile of the speaker. Is it so difficult to say that I want something instead of I need it? I don't know—the word want seems to connote a willingness to negotiate. For after all, I may want a new car, but if you gave me a bus pass, it still would be helpful but if I need a new car, it sounds like I might be offended by a lesser offer. Words do get in the way. Just ask anybody negotiating a treaty for peace.

3. And finally, the reason to change our needs to wants—*it prepares us for how the corporation really works.* Because the fact of the matter is, we never get what we need, we sometimes get what we want, but *we always get what's next.* That's right. Progress has been set in motion and you can either hinder it or help it. The chances that you're going to change it are slim. Anyone who is in a position of wanting instead of needing has the pliability to consider using what's next. Perhaps we all wish life was really a democracy where input is received, discussion ensues, motions are made and votes are taken. But after all, it is not that

way. Living is a determined motion that gathers steam through time, chance and often random chaos, tumbling down the hill towards us, offering a warning of its intention, encouraging us to either run ahead or jump on board, but certainly not averse to rolling right over the top of us.

We always get what's next. It's the only thing that we can count on. If what's next intrigues us, if we really believe that good and prospering can come out of anything through a willingness to adjust and adapt, then there is nothing that can destroy or defeat us. If we stand in the way of the natural progress of the corporation of the universe, holding up a placard to advertise our need, we will be struck down by the wheels of progress.

There is nothing wrong with running along with the natural flow of existence and panting out your wishes, as long as you keep up and follow pace. If you stand in the way and demand attention to your need, no matter how worthy the cause or request may be, you will be trampled by the feet of those who are intelligent enough to stay up with the gravy train.

And of course, avoid greatest form of neediness—the assertion that reality is hard. Reality isn't anything. It's just what's next.

Living a legendary life demands that we change the circumstances of our planet by participating instead of demanding.

You will never get what you need.

You sometimes get what you want.

And you always get what's next.

Find your place. Get in the flow and then go.

It makes a whole lot more sense.

-Sitting Three-
ISA

There is a trio of troubled troubadours who raise their ugly heads to sing off-key tunes, causing all of humanity to suffer in the listening. They tour together. They only believe in each other, and they foster the conditions causing all the pain experienced on the planet that we have called Earth.

Pretty dramatic beginning, don't you think? Now that I have your attention, let me introduce these dunderheads of defeat. The mother's name is *insecurity*. She hounds, pecks and nags to bring about her will. That will is very simple: to establish the need for love rather than a love relationship. She points out flaws and never forgives them. She projects an image of us in the mirror that is never to our favor. She discourages all attempts at improvement in favor of complaining. She leaves her household barren of basic human confidence.

And then she turns to her sister, *superstition*, to explain the rules of operation. And superstition is nothing if not a pernicious explainer. Superstition lays the groundwork for the reasoning behind all the insecurity. Superstition fosters the notion that there are supernatural reasons for the most natural of events. Superstition binds the human heart in grave clothes for future entombment. Superstition warns of dangers which are never realized and promotes prejudices for the alleged protection and purification of all. Superstition insists upon promoting ritual over rhyme, practice over discovery and dogma over true belief.

And then, she invites the big brother to come in to seal the deal.

His name is *arrogance*. Arrogance has an excuse for everything. He is the guardian of superstition and insecurity, protecting them from knowledge and learning. Arrogance is clothed in fakery and armed with ignorance. Arrogance flexes its muscle to prove superiority. Arrogance is the enforcer of all that makes us insecure and all that causes us to revere the superstitious.

The trio rampage through the human fold like a wolf at night, destroying all semblance of innocence and all sensation of protection. They are the ravagers of passion and the mockers of simplicity. They fear no one but continue their mission of mayhem, seemingly unchecked by any mortal force.

Their only weakness is that they don't seem to be able to function alone and when separated, the true essence of their nature shines through, exposing them for who they are.

Insecurity—a jealous child.

Superstition—a baffled bungler of misinformation.

Arrogance—an ignorant brute.

So insecurity is very careful to cling to superstition, and superstition cannot exist without arrogance.

Fortunately for all human beings great and small, there is a threesome that counters the efforts of this diabolical trio.

Standing firmly and strongly in an intelligent profile against the mother of insecurity is *acceptance*. Acceptance is the perfect counter against all insecurity because it dismisses the notion that there is an ultimate look, idea or even way of things. Acceptance accepts. First, ourselves—for who we are. And then, with that tremendous boost of confidence, allows for a universal acceptance of difference in others. Acceptance is the notion that we are of value only as long as we are not constantly trying to reinvent ourselves but instead work with the package provided.

Logic has been summoned to counteract superstition. Logic rarely has an opinion, but poses the well-placed and timed question to dispel false witness. Logic just wants to know if there is any history to the proposed action and if there is any future to practicing the suggested behavior. Logic desires evidence. Although logic has a reputation for being an unbeliever, it has been through the logical action of spiritual souls that the planet Earth has been able to dismiss the errant philosophies that have brought us near the brink of destruction. Can there be anything more god-like than the probing question that splits the darkness and demands, "Let there be light?" Logic becomes faith when enacted by people of passion.

And finally, there is *humility*, which, for some odd reason, has gained a reputation for being weak-willed and paper thin in its determination. Humility is merely a profile taken by any well-traveled, intelligent soul who knows there is always more to learn. Humility feels no need to supersede the will of others, but only wishes to be a part of the whole.

As in the case of insecurity, superstition and arrogance, our three friends of acceptance, logic and humility gain strength through one another.

Leading a legendary life is a decision to accept who we are and the status of those around us, while we are logically requesting an explanation for events, and humbly placing ourselves in the flow of humanity instead of an arrogant seat of power above others.

The trio of troublers: insecurity, superstition and arrogance.

The trinity of triumph: acceptance, logic and humility.

Be certain of this: you will belong to one family or another. This, a certainty.

-Sitting Four-
The Whore of Babble-On

So little Suzy or little Brian bring their picture to Mommy and Daddy for approval. On the sheet of paper are seven lines drawn in various colors of Crayola by a young person with a tiny hand. So what do Mommy and Daddy say?

"Oh, it's beautiful! It's the most glorious picture I've ever seen! You have such a talent! You're gonna grow up to be an artist! Let's hang it here on the wall. Can you make another one for Grandma and Grandpa?"

Are the comments sincere? Perhaps. Truthful? Not completely. Helpful? No. What is the value of unfounded praise lavished upon our children?

Because it is much easier to praise than it is to perfect.

So little Suzy or Brian skip away as we look on, totally convinced we have done a noble and superior job of parenting.

Babble.

Can anyone tell me what would be wrong with looking at the picture that Suzy or little Brian drew and asking them what they were trying to portray while pointing

33

out, in a positive tone, where we actually can see that in the picture? In other words, "That line right there does look like a rainbow. Good job. Now, go make some more lines like that, and use the colors that are in a rainbow."

Babbling on in false praise to our younger generation, when we know that very soon they will be harangued by schoolyard competition, classroom demands, and ultimately by the workplace grind, is not only worthless, but in the final scheme of things, mean-spirited. We are generating an offspring of "praise-whores"—people who cannot function unless they are continually encouraged by the approval of others.

Here's the problem: if everyone needs approval, at least half of us at any given time are not satisfied. Someone has to be speaking and someone has to be receiving, am I right? Just as neediness betrays us, a thirst for praise makes us vulnerable to all sorts of aggravations and con artists. I predict that promoting self-esteem is going to be ridiculed by the next generation that has suffered from dependence upon self-worth to achieve personal value.

It is the *Whore of Babble-On.*

34

I know we want to edify one another, but really, the best way we can do so is to use encouragement when quality is established and direction when improvement is required.

In the Bible it tells the story of Cain and Abel and how Cain felt slighted because he was not given the positive reinforcement for his gift that was provided to his brother, Abel. We hear the voice of the God speaking to Cain, saying, "If you do well, won't you be accepted?"

Exactly. Concerted effort affords opportunity to shine. Can we stop issuing certificates of participation? I'm sorry. Merely participating does not warrant recognition.

Too much babble just creates rabble lending itself to a discontented populace that has no legitimate evidence of its own ability but rather, a drawer-full of commendations for merely showing up. If this rhetoric were actually beneficial, I would remain silent. But we are not better people because we praise each other. Our children are not more industrious because we applaud all of their attempts. Test scores are not rising because teachers painstakingly point out tiny increments of improvement. Sports teams are not achieving greater quality because coaches accept sub-par performances. The verdict is in. *Self-esteem perpetuated by using supportive language instead of the opportunity for achievement is vacant of lasting value.*

For then the worst atrocity unfolds: these folks arrive into the marketplace of our country anticipating ongoing positive acclamation to discover that corporate America only honors one conclusion—productivity at the bottom line.

When will we finally understand that the only true builder of self-esteem is the realistic reward that is acquired by equivalent effort? Living a legendary life is brushing aside the flattery that is so readily available in this day and age and opting for candid assessment on performance. No, it will not always be a rousing report. It will not always be warm and fuzzy.

But it will always be factual and useful.

Suzy and Brian were not born needy. They were born inquisitive. We silence their inquisitive nature by telling them they are all right the way they are. They don't want that. They want to find out how to do better.

It isn't like we don't do it in some areas of their lives. We don't let them mispronounce words to keep from offending

36

them. We don't permit them to continue to crawl because we fear we'll frustrate them by asking them to walk. We don't tolerate them pooping in their diapers with hopes that one day they'll motivate themselves toward the toilet. We guide them in the ways that will bring true prosperity to every area of their being—heart, soul, mind and strength.

So why do we feel the need in areas of ego to be misleading and ingenuous?

Honest to God, Brian and Suzy would be more receptive to us as parents if we would take two more minutes to explain to them how a rainbow really looks so they could draw one. No one is asking you to be cruel. No one is suggesting blatant critique.

Realistic assessment.

My God, can't we all benefit from that? A legendary life is an existence that is not afraid to be graded on the work provided, with the contention that C's can become B's and even that F's can become D's; progress can be made through truthful evaluation.

As long as the Whore of Babble-On is at work in a society, we will raise a generation addicted to approval.

Did Edison make the light bulb to get a pat on the head? Is it really approval that caused Lincoln to free the slaves? Is it applause that motivated Martin Luther King, Jr. as he marched from Selma to Birmingham?

If we think that by gaining a consensus of accolade that we make any progress in our lives, we deny the sacrifice of all artisans and diplomats through the ages who have given up their need for personal appreciation to better the life of humankind.

Let's turn down the noise. Let's turn up the voice of reason and allow ourselves the privilege of legitimately succeeding without ploy. Don't be surprised that if we continue to teach ourselves and our children to whore to achieve necessary attention, that the obvious end result will be the prostituting of true talent, true ability and true passion to settle for lesser effort, lesser emotion and lesser intensity.

Living a legendary life is rejecting false acclaim in favor of lasting satisfaction.

-Sitting Five-
The Art of Flaunting

She stood as tall and as sturdy as she could when knees are knocking. Her daddy thought it was a good idea that she play her violin for her G-Pop—that being a clever family name for Grandpa.

I'm G-Pop.

Let me take a quick sidebar here and say that the violin is so much like the rest of life—in the hands of someone who is excellent, well-practiced and dexterous, it can be a lovely instrument. In everybody else's hands, it has a similar effect on a gathering of people to the machete, in the sense that we all should be terrified of the instrument's nature to produce death and mayhem, but for some inexplicable reason, we are frozen, too afraid to run away.

That being said, I return to my story.

I believe the goal of the evening's offering was *Jingle Bells*. I say this not by recognition of the performance rendered, but by the fact that my son announced the title following the debacle. At the end of the piece, (which seems accurate since we certainly never heard the whole song) we all applauded nicely—kindly. She left the room and then, we, being particularly notorious adults, giggled a bit amongst ourselves, not knowing that the little lass lurked around the corner, listening in on our conversation.

In a few moments she came upstairs with tears in her eyes, debunked, decried and deflowered by having overheard our more candid reviews of her effort. We all felt bad.

But what astounded me was that although she was just six years old, and although she knew that she didn't sound like Perleman, she was greatly offended.

I thought, "What exactly is bothering her?"

Oh, I know we all despise being laughed at, but "laugh" is really a good word. Because it's okay to laugh with, and laugh for and laugh in and laugh out and laugh toward or even, I suppose, laugh of (whatever that would be,) but we're just not supposed to laugh at, especially if it is at creatures sporting skin and pumping blood (although I guess family pets are an exception.)

Yes, we all felt a little guilty about having hurt the young lady's feelings, but she seemed to feel no guilt about having mutilated a great American classic. Being a novice, she should have been taught and prepared to be received as one.

Let me offer an alternative. How disarming would it be to walk into a room and say, "You'll never guess what I just did!" and then to tell a story on yourself—a story in which you confess some form of ineptness. I mean, what would really have happened if this little girl had reached the end of her song, turned to us all, smiled and said, "Gee, that was just not very good, was it?"

My dear God, we would have lavished her with hugs, kisses and probably any flavor of ice cream she would dare to dream up. It is so astounding to me that we think that our best defense against criticism is to select haughtiness or pride.

There is an art to flaunting. The first step in acquiring this art is to understand that the first mile on any journey is a given. In this day and age we are forced to feign appreciation for services that should just be rendered. Not realistic to the function of how the universe really operates.

Everyone is compelled to go the first mile. Everyone must work. Yet we continue to insist on praises and raises for merely adequate job performance. And when we make mistakes we become sensitive if our boss is critical of us.

The first mile is a given. Oh, yes, I already said that.

When we've done that which is expected of us, we should take the intelligent stance of shrugging our shoulders and stating to the entire room, "Oh well, that wasn't very much, now, was it?"

This self-effacing selection of words enables us, dare I say, *empowers* us to be able to propel on to the second mile, where things really do happen and human spirits can soar to new heights of grandeur.

What is it in our species that is afraid to make mistakes and then just flaunt them?

"Guess what happened on my way to the bathroom? I nearly slipped and fell and killed myself! But thank God, I caught myself on the chair. Maybe I should hire a bodyguard to protect me from my own toilet trips."

What is the end result of this statement? What does the average human being garner from sharing humorously and humbly about their errors and flaunting them? Yes. Flaunting them for all to hear, for all to see, so that it gives us credibility both as a fellow-traveler and even more, as a trusted companion who would never consider covering up error.

The true art of living a legendary life is flaunting your mistakes so you're always laughing with others instead of setting up grandiose falls in the future over little cover-ups now.

There is just power to the art of flaunting mistakes. For as I said, the true goal of every human being is to set up a scenario where it is possible, even feasible, to exceed expectation. If we continue to live in a world where the mediocre is fastidiously accepted, regarded as effort, we will back our way into such a sludge of poverty and ignorance that we will spin our wheels for decades trying to get out of the mud.

It's not so much that someone needs to stand up and say the emperor has no clothes, as it is that the emperor, if he wants to continue to rule, must realize his own nakedness, recognize the stupidity of being manipulated and flaunt his mistake—realize, advertise and energize.

Ask yourself: do you really want people working with you and for you who make mistakes and keep you in the dark about them until those errors have denigrated to tragedy? Or do you want to work with folks who immediately acquiesce to their own failings and allow precious time to correct the small bunglings long before they ring the death-knell of failure? It's what the old-timers used to call "'fessin'.'" And I, for one, would love to see not only the term, but the practice reinstated in our everyday lives. Because only when we're living a life of "fessin" do we get the extra bump for the outstanding blessings.

For it is in the first mile of life that I do what I am told and what is required and what I am paid to achieve. It is only in the second mile that the more creative parts of my personality come forward. It is in the second mile that I gain control of my own life and cease to be just a paid consumer and become an ingenious thinker.

But to do this, we must be willing to gain credibility by a) flaunting our mistakes so that people will know we will never be party to an attempt to cover-up; b) keep a natural humility about ourselves in recognizing that our first-mile efforts are bare-minimum activity; and c) create a climate where we are recognized as the type of individual who will not be satisfied until the work is improved. And I am not talking about perfected. I am speaking of just a natural surge toward enlightenment.

If we flaunt our mistakes and laugh at ourselves and give permission to the entire scope of humanity to join us, we actually will hear much less ridicule coming our way. We will have a series of individuals— dare I call them the "concerned-watches–a-lot-of-daytime-television-amateur-psychologist-and-wants-to-make-sure-everybody-gets-a-fair-shake" sorts—who will come behind our self-deprecation and try to reinforce what they determine to be our ailing self-esteem with words of encouragement. My God. Who knows? Maybe even chicken soup.

Living a legendary life is getting to the task that has been provided, laughing heartily at the mistakes along the way, completing the required agenda and then looking for opportunities to motivate a second mile of action that is of our selection and our unction.

Be smart. Everyone knows the story of Adam and Eve. Every culture, in some form, has a similar story, where mankind opened Pandora's Box through arrogance and stupidity and unleashed havoc on the planet. But Adam and Eve were never punished for eating an apple or for any fruit consumption, for that matter. The sin of Adam and Eve is the sin of our species, and that is the craftiness of cover-up instead of the art of flaunting mistakes. Larry did not ask them why they ate the fruit they weren't supposed to eat. He asked them why they were hiding from him.

Yes. Why are we hiding? My God, let me find my mistake, put a big, red bow on it and present it to mankind while I still have the power to spin the tale of the error and the laughter about its unfolding. Otherwise, I will find myself, like so many people in history who were never punished for their crimes, but suffered both personally and historically for the cover-up.

As horrible as the killing of six million Jews by a German madman may be, the fact that the slimy wad of human skin did it secretly, without conscience without the awareness of the majority of his own people, is even more deplorable.

The fact that a political party broke into another political party's headquarters to gain access to information is a bit smarmy, but nothing in comparison to the leader of that party denying any awareness of the plan, deceiving the nation, and eventually forfeiting the honor of holding the greatest office in our land.

A little six-year-old girl who plays a ragged rendition of *Jingle Bells*, who is not aware of her own limitations, but rather expects an ongoing flood of unrealistic praise, may be comforted for a moment, but will eventually aggravate a whole house of normally genial human beings.

You can agree or you can disagree. And if you disagree and you're wrong, I hope you will be smart enough to flaunt your mistake. And if I'm wrong, watch out. Because I'll be bringing a marching band, fourteen majorettes and a dancing bear to flaunt mine.

Oh, by the way, I will probably also bring refreshments.

-Sitting Six-
From Whence

"Where did *that* come from?" Probably one of the more common questions asked in everyday life. Do you think we would be happier if we weren't constantly bewildered by the stuff that crosses our path?

Why did the car pick today to break down? Why is my wife or husband in such a bad mood?

Why did the school call today of all days to tell me about my child's grades? Why is the boss cutting benefits on the health insurance program?

Lacking understanding often causes us to utter the screaming question, "why?" into a vast cavern of nothingness. For after all, we don't believe we're going to get an answer, which only lends itself to greater frustration.

Ah, there's the word. Frustration. For all dilemmas in life are a blending of circumstance and frustration spawning offspring that seem to always stimulate the same reaction. In other words, it is not a single event that brings difficulty or blessing into our lives, but how that event blends with existing levels of frustration or, may I add at this point, willingness.

I contend that these two words are opposites. Frustration is the opposite of willingness. When we are no longer willing to adjust, some form of frustration inhabits our soul. When we have grown weary of the tedium of frustration, we allow some measure of willingness to seep back into play.

Circumstances *exist.* To think that circumstances control our destiny is the reason that so many people are fearful and miserable in their daily flow. Circumstance is one-half of a formula that creates a compound, either compounding our success, or compounding our difficulty.

From whence comes fear? How about joy? How about problems? How about pain? How about mercy? How about evil?

There is no single occurrence that produces any of these conclusions. What I'm saying is, there's no such thing as existing evil. But when an action is mingled with an ongoing frustration, it can and does produce evil.

Joy also does not exist by itself. But when a happening is mingled with some human willingness, it can and does produce joy.

It's time for our own little adventure into the mysterious impasse called the human heart—taking a look at the different elements of frustration and willingness, to see how they combine to form the perceptions in our lives.

So what are the varieties of frustration?

Frustration has five symptoms, some of them obvious and others a bit surprising.

1. Anticipation. It connotes a bit of excitement. But anticipation is more often an impatient, gnawing need. It is one of those demanding emotions rather than a flexible one. Emotions that turn to stone lead to frustration. Emotions that remain rubber lend themselves to willingness.

2. Confusion. There is an arrogance to this one. Confusion assumes that many things are difficult to understand and therefore often hurls us into the pit of despair. Valuable confusion should lead to the question, "I don't understand, would you please explain?" But most confusion ends up in a statement rather than a question— "This is just too hard to understand"—soil for the growth of frustration.

3. ***Conviction.*** Belief is toted as an ever-positive presence in our culture. But beliefs should be expansive, like a man and woman marrying and buying a two-bedroom house, knowing that with the addition of children, more rooms will have to be added on. When beliefs become convictions, they lose the ability to be tugged on by discovery to become bigger and more inclusive. Conviction by its very nature assumes that things are a certain way, should be a certain way and should remain that way. It is a petrie dish for breeding frustration.

4. ***Positive thinking.*** The universe is negatively charged. It is comical to think that by taking a couple of synapses from my brain and triggering them with platitudes, I can change the ongoing avalanche of events in my world. Positive thinking is wonderful at establishing direction and horrible at adjusting to the course of change. It is audacious and perhaps pugnacious to try to change our destiny by speaking simple phrases of hope in the midst of despair when what is needed is involvement and good, old-fashioned elbow grease. My experience with positive thinkers is that they always end up positively baffled by why things did not work out the way they claimed or spoke them into being. They tend to be the

kindling wood for the fires of all frustrations.

5. And finally, ***hope.*** There is a great book that says "hope deferred makes the heart sick." And, may I add, frustrated. Having faith may be the absence of foresight, but hope needs to be graced by wisdom and intelligence to be viable. Otherwise, it's just wishing. People who just wish are constantly disappointed and dangerously teetering on a great chasm of frustration.

So, as you can see, we often consider frustration to be the end result of trials like resentment, anger, fear, pain, difficulty and evil, when actually, these are the compounds remaining when we link the five attitudes above with the natural circumstances of life.

Let me stop talking in circles here and be more specific. Jane, having just attended a seminar conducted by her company on positive thinking, arrived in the parking lot to discover she had a flat tire.

Reaching for her phone to call AAA, a friend nearby piped up, "Is that what we learned in the seminar?"

Jane paused to consider. How did what she learned in the seminar apply to this situation? She certainly felt the need to remain positive and to not accept the flat tire as part of her day, but rather a distraction that needed to be swatted away by reinforcing her own thinking with influential language and upgraded energy.

The friend patted her on the back and headed for his car. "Good luck, Jane. But stay the course."

Jane was willing to stay the course, she just didn't know what the course was. Some confusion was at work. She valued her convictions. While she was deliberating, a young man walked up to her and asked if she needed any help. Her reply was, "I'm not sure."

He smiled and said, "Well, when will you be sure?"

She thanked him, but felt it was premature to try to resolve the problem until she understood what exactly the situation was and why it had come into her life.

A few minutes later, another young man approached. "What 'cha doing?" he asked.

"Trying to decide what to do about this situation," she replied.

The young man said, "Well, why you're deciding, why don't you reach into your wallet and pull out all your cash and credit cards and give them to me."

He pulled a knife. Jane did as the young man requested, not feeling any need to deliberate her choices.

After the young man departed, she called the police, later lamenting to the officer, "Why did this happen to me?"

It is really quite simple. Circumstance mingled with frustration always produces conflict. That even goes for circumstances that were intended to be good, which were either overlooked or stalled by indecision, producing strife.

If you will allow me to review for a moment, nothing that happens in our life that is negative is caused by an event or a circumstance. Even the tragedies in our journey are in themselves not isolated actions producing evil. It all depends on what they're blended with, what we mingle with our life occurrences to create a new compound, be it born of frustration or born of willingness.

So now that we know the five compounds that breed frustration, what are the five elements that create the compounds that welcome success?

1. Questioning. "If any of you lack wisdom, ask." Any questioning individual will receive a myriad of possible answers. Understandably, this can be frustrating in

54

itself. But it is in the multitude of counselors that we gain both time and insight to find a way to turn all circumstances into bounty. The well-formed question is the greatest defense to frustration. Frustration assumes. The mere presence of a question admits the desire for input and foils frustration.

2. Humor. Good cheer is one of the few ways that we can actually battle wrong. Mankind has tried confrontation, conversation and contemplation and this trio has left us bedraggled, warring with each other. Just the ability to laugh, first at oneself, then at the humorless circumstances in front of us, and finally, in the face of threatening disaster, buys the necessary time for the circumstances to evolve. I think humor is the true definition of turning the other cheek. Not the self-righteous posturing of superiority that makes somebody want to hit you again, but rather the humble, jocular approach that admits vulnerability, while establishing a natural advantage by bringing laughter to a tangled turmoil.

3. Reasoning. Is there a danger in jumping to conclusions in life? Have we ever thought that something was one way and the next moment it turned out to be different? Although these are rhetorical questions, I'm going to go ahead and say "yes." Before we continue to assume that we know what has really happened, perhaps five or six seconds of reasoning, or even asking someone else's opinion might divulge information. There is just such a power in saying, "Okay. Let's count to ten here and see if we really understand what's going on." I often feel that problems are compounded by premature solutions. Over-reaction is the true enemy of resolution and opinions are about as valuable as a leaky cup in the middle of the desert. Honestly, most of the time it's not what we feel is going on that's important, but rather allowing for a spate of time for information to come in and reasoning to have a chance to wipe away at least part of the frustration before we even start to address the rest.

4. *Distraction.* I always thought distraction was a negative state. But can there be anything more mature or intelligent than a selected distraction in the middle of what we consider to be an unfortunate turn of affairs? If our true enemy is frustration mingling with occurrence to create a compounding of difficulty, then anything that would come along to get our minds off the process of becoming frustrated is a godsend. In other words, on our way to slay the dragon, let's stop off for some distraction. Time is not our enemy—not when it buys us space to keep from becoming frustrated juggernauts on the way to our own destruction. I have often been sipping a bowl of soup while the world around me seemed to be falling apart. Upon finishing the last mouthful, I discovered that the sky was not actually falling, just making a natural adjustment needed to improve my status. If I had jumped in and gotten frustrated, I could have very easily screwed it up. And soup tastes better.

5. Finally, the fifth element that goes into the making of success is *relinquishment.* What is really worth fighting for? I just don't know, do you? Oh, I can certainly recite a series of words from a holy lexicon that seem to espouse noble causes for crusades, but are they? Often in life, bullies will come along and want to steal the ball from us. If we can just remember that bullies have two major downfalls, the first and most obvious being that they are overbearing jerks that are willing to do anything to control the situation. This particular flaw infuriates us because none of us want to be manipulated. But we must take into consideration the second foible of all bullies: because they're

attention span is similar to that of a horny gnat, they grow bored easily. Soon they abandon the ball, leaving it for general availability. We can, at that point, just simply walk up and retrieve it. Because more often than not, they don't even know how to play with the ball.

Relinquish. Sometimes in life, the most intelligent thing to do is to give it up for a season to get it back forever. There is an arrogance and frustration that keeps us from relinquishing what *just can't be* in order to gain what *truly might be.*

So if you will, with all of this in mind, let me set in motion some possibilities.

Shall we return to our dear friend Jane? Facts are, Jane just had a flat tire. It wasn't a personal attack, nor a test of her newfound positive prowess. But because Jane took the circumstances of a flat tire and added the frustrations of positive thinking and confusion, she compounded her situation and became a victim of crime, an action of evil.

A man goes to the doctor and receives diagnoses of cancer. This is real. But he chooses to add the frustration of anticipation and on the way home, has a rise in blood pressure, a stroke and ends up in the hospital, incapacitated. It would seem that this man was having the trials of Job, when really, he sacrificed his opportunity to receive treatment for his cancer by anticipating his demise and inviting debilitation.

On the other hand, Jack received news that he was about to lose his job. Jack, being an astute fellow, knew that rumors were rampant in his company, so rather than being frustrated, he waited for a few minutes, asked a couple of questions and sure enough, found out that he was indeed losing his job—because his job was being phased out and he was being promoted to another department with a salary increase. Refusing frustration, he also avoided the embarrassment of confronting his bosses and making a fool of himself.

All fear, difficulty, resentment and evil come from frustration being added to the normal circumstances of life to compound iniquity. All mercy, success, blessing, discovery, faith and joy transpire when the elements of willingness are offered in moments of confusing circumstance.

From whence come the blessings in our life? When we add willingness to the passing circumstances, we create a legendary juncture for ourselves. From whence come the evil and difficulties in our life? When we allow the frustrations to compound our tribulations to create monsters never foreseen.

A legendary life. Putting the right elements together to create the right compounds.

-Sitting Seven-
The Danger of PONDering

Once we realize that we are being observed, heightening our awareness of our own lives and we stop pursuing the leaden notion that something good is just *going* to happen to us, we are ready to take ourselves into the mix.

And there, it all boils down to this "big pond-little pond" thing.

There are so many sayings that we parrot everyday without giving them a second thought. One of those is "Oh, he's just a big fish in a little pond." The concept? Take the risk of being a little fish in a big pond, competing with all the sharks in the water.

But is that an ideal?

Thus we have the title of this sitting: the Danger of PONDering.

Because we feel we should not be content with where we are, we live dissatisfied lives. In other words, if all things were equal, we would be further along than we are.

If all things were balanced, our boss would have given us that promotion.

If everything had been ordained, I would have married *him.*

Just a few more breaks and my kids would have won the award.

We're always trying to jump ponds—PONDering ourselves off to nagging aggravations of misgiving. It creates a national mood. Have you ever asked yourself why people shopping in a mall are sullen?

As many people as the plague may have killed in 1918, it is a pittance compared to the emotional death toll on human life brought on by the *I've been cheated* disease.

Living a legendary life is facing reality without opinion.

No one is strategically placed in the planet scheme but we will never change our surroundings by denying them.

There is nothing wrong with being a big fish in a little pond, unless your goal is to gobble up your neighbors.

A big fish in a little pond can be legendary.

A big fish in a little pond can be a benefactor.

A big fish in a little pond can be instrumental in improving the quality of life.

A big fish in a little pond can instigate cleaning up the pond. A big fish in a little pond is in a better position to see the whole pond.

A big fish in a little pond can be a source of strength to the weaker.

Function. Do we require more?

We are so frightened of the possibility that our lives may be just what they appear to be. What if they are? What if the next how-to book isn't going to transform us into the multi-millionaire, social dynamo or business tycoon that is promised on the dust cover?

What if our life is exactly what it is? And all the pond-jumping or PONDering that we do merely duplicates the same set of circumstances, just in a larger, foreign environment?

If your life ended up being exactly what it is now, and if that disappoints you, are you being duped? Please don't be offended or misunderstand. We have woven a tangled web for ourselves through this dangerous habit of "pond jumping." Can we truthfully improve our lives by changing our external environment?

Often we're not happy in the pond we came from and even less fulfilled in the pond we've jumped into.

If you will allow me, the problem is not the pond. The problem is there's something fishy—our reasoning.

A sidebar—certainly there are ponds we must leave. When life is threatened, emotion stifled, mind controlled, spirit quenched, and body harmed—it is time to swim away.

But if these problems do not exist and we are just hypnotized by repetition, we must stop PONDering, and therefore pandering, to philosophies which, although commonly accepted, have not been thoroughly tested, at least not for us.

Living a legendary life is the ability to function in such a way that you can illuminate your own path, generate your own energy and fulfill your own goals to such an extent that the fallout from the process radiates to the people in the world around you.

No one or no place is going to provide the impetus for you to be happy. This is why religion is stale in the banquet of everyday conflict. This is why politics fails to deliver us from the evil that besets us because both realms—religion and politics—depend on manufacturing fear to rattle us into adopting their cause. But when the storm clouds pass, the pressure subsides and the fear of earthly confrontation or eternal damnation is diminished, then we are left with the ongoing drizzle of dreary drone, minus inspiration.

We require something else.

We require a motivator that is not fear-based.

We require a realization that our pond is where we live and it is fine and it is meant to become the very best that we can possibly make it.

You may ask—where is the motivation to become larger? But I ask you—since when does our motivation amount to a hill of beans difference as to the conclusion of how the rewards of life are passed along? There isn't a person reading this book who doesn't understand that good things happen to bad people and bad things happen to good people, and most of the time, nothing happens to everybody.

So how do we feel about that? How do we feel about a world that establishes order even when that order is insensitive to our needs? How do we feel about that negatively charged universe? How do we function on a planet that feels no particular responsibility to entertain us, but will allow us to vegetate, if we succumb, until we eke away all the valuable moments of our passage?

If life were naturally exciting, we could just allow it to wash over us. Facts are, life without tweaking is achingly boring and interminably lengthy.

Unless we accept our pond and work within it, we will fall into the dangerous pattern of believing that finding another place of growth will actually stimulate us to grow. The dreaded "place over purpose." It's a killer.

Good news, my friends. We are in charge of our growth. We are also susceptible to stunting it.

The glory of the universe is that our Creator, or the creative force, or whatever you believe it may be, chooses not to interfere in the mechanism that propels us.

Of course, that does mean we must show up and tweak our own pond situation.

So the question remains: what's wrong with pond jumping? What is the danger of moving about like Goldilocks trying to find the perfect bed?

The danger: when too many people vie to occupy the same space, there is always war.

I remember as a young boy, being told about the population explosion—how the world was becoming over-crowded. Then I drove across miles and miles of prairie, plains, meadows and desert with nary a soul in sight for hours.

You see, the problem is not that the world is crowded. The problem is not that the road to success is jammed. The problem is that the parts of the world that everybody wants, and the roads to success which are generally traversed, are always shoulder-to-shoulder and the prairies and less traveled roads to success are mainly vacant, waiting for anyone who will come and take the time to stake a claim and carve out a Promised Land.

Is Hollywood the only location to make movies? How about your town?

Is New York the only center for business? How about your idea?

Is Washington D.C. the best place to create political change? How about your city council?

Here's to doing swimmingly in our own pond!

-Sitting Eight-
It's Not Really Giving

Poverty just does not go away—really has no intention of departing and has nests all over the world. We've attempted campaigns to eliminate poverty in our lifetime, to address the issue, and basically, have succeeded in advertising its existence fairly well, but not eliminating its presence.

What is the source of poverty?

Is it genetic? If, by genetic, you mean does it run in families, well, certainly you'd have to say "yes" to that. If by genetic you mean is there a predisposition in certain cultures toward falling into the poverty cycle? Undoubtedly. If by genetic, you mean it is beyond our escaping because of the particular formation and construction of a gene pool, then no.

For after all, everyone on the planet is trying to wriggle out of their genes, get rid of the loafers and dress for success.

But I think we all pretty well agree. The poor aren't going away any time soon.

The goal? Don't plead poverty and therefore join the ranks. I think there is little in life that is more disgusting than people who pretend like they have no resource simply because they aren't able to grant themselves a favored delicacy.

Poverty is real and shouldn't be mocked by those who are just having budgeting concerns or priority checks and want to appear temporarily destitute.

So how do we avoid poverty?

I think we have to get rid of the word "giving," especially as it pertains to our personal finance. When we talk about giving, there is a danger of trying to appear noble and express superiority by acting like "we really want to give and they don't."

But after all, it really isn't giving.

The process by which we take what we have and place it into the hands of other people who don't is not an act of charity. It really is returning.

I do not agree with the practice of tithing on command or fulfilling pledges. It makes us too self-righteous, and ultimately, much too stingy. For honestly, I've never met a person that is swelled with personal pride who is not also miserly, although they, themselves, would be oblivious to the fault.

What I discovered in the pursuit of a legendary life is, there is just stuff, and even money, in my life that lies in a no man's land of inactivity. I keep it around, mingling sentimentality with laziness to create an evolution—goods become stuff, which begets storage, culminating in junk. Isn't it amazing that we really feel no guilt about accumulating things for no purpose? I, for instance, seem to have no remorse whatsoever about throwing my pocket change into a jar to later give to a grandchild so he or she can buy another over-the-top gift that was barely expensive enough to become a blip on the radar screen.

I recently looked in my closet at the array of clothes I've accumulated through both the process of gifts and weight loss up and down. Having a few minutes of spare time, I made a quick count and realized that nearly 62% of my clothing is ignored and closeted to its own devices. I might actually wear some of those things later on, but chances are I will pass over them to favor a more common outfit. (I do not know why certain clothes become our favorites—the way they fit, the way we think they look, their color, their ease in cleaning, or just that we did some really neat stuff in them and every time we wear them we feel that "old black magic." But I know that about 62% of my clothing is ignored to the point of abandonment.)

Now here's the question: am I willing to give up that 62% of my clothes, leaving my closet temporarily depleted thus making me feel momentarily a bit less prosperous?

The answer to that question is no. I'm a human being. I don't want to give up anything. Can I take my change, put it in a jar and every two weeks, turn it into dollar bills and give it to someone close by that would benefit with an extra gallon of milk, a pack of baloney or a dozen eggs? No, because then I don't have it anymore. It steals my sense of plenty and places me in a position of adequacy.

But facts are, I can train myself to return back to life the things that I presently am not using, with the stipulation that if I ever need them again, life promises to replenish my storehouse. I can't give away my clothes. But I can return them back into the main stream because they don't fit or weren't the right color, or just didn't hang right. I mean, we do it at Christmas. We return gifts all the time. Or we pass them on to another person. Why not in our everyday lives?

How much weight would we lose in a year if we just returned to somebody else the extra food that other people just give to us? I know your friend picked up an extra donut on the way to work and they were thinking of you, but, for God's sakes, you just finished a 42-pound blueberry muffin with your coffee! I'm not talking about whether you want the donut, or whether you even need the donut. I'm speaking logically here—pass it on. Return it. Not to the person who gave it to you, but to the person who runs in late and didn't get breakfast.

Do you really need the change to buy another useless present for someone, or can you give up your change? And I'm not speaking of the United Way. I'm talking about the people in your path—those individuals who have managed to burst through your three square feet of humanity, who obviously have points of need. How many times do we go to a restaurant and ask for a doggy bag or a to-go box, stick it in the refrigerator and find it two weeks later, growing the most gruesome head of green hair? Get your food in the to-go box, make a quick stop on the way home, send your teenage kid to the door to deliver the extra food to someone who can't get out, but might like a smidgen of left-over Texi-Mexi Chicken smothered in something or other.

You see, it's not giving. It's merely returning those things that have no immediate value to us.

As a reader you may be saying, "You're just describing what was taught to us in kindergarten—the principle of sharing."

But with sharing, we were taught to give it away before we had even decided if we wanted the whole thing. That's not it. I am saying that the average family could feed a whole second family for a week off of the leftover food that rots in our refrigerator and the morsels that dry out in our cupboards.

Not giving. Not sharing.

Returning.

"Here. I'm not using this."

I think as long as we try to become giving people, that laziness, oblivion or self-righteousness will impede our progress.

If it is in your hand, and not in your use, return it. It is as simple as that. You will find that you will become known as a giving person. You will find that it may even tally up to be more than your church tithe or your club dues or your recent pledge to charity. But it won't feel sacrificial in the least.

I know there are those people who believe that unless it's sacrificial giving it's not any good. We can only hope that they die soon. Human sacrifice in any way, shape and form is an abomination to all the absolutes of the universe and anything that might truly be holy.

Larry doesn't want your sacrifice. Larry wants you in the flow. Larry wants you thinking. Aren't we just better when we're thinking? Aren't we better when we consider what to do with something rather than tucking it away for a rainy day? You don't need anything for a rainy day but an umbrella. Go buy one and return the rest of what you're not using, what you don't want, or those things that seem to have escaped your fancy, to the nearest neighbor and let it trickle down.

It's not really giving. It is returning.

Living a legendary life is not finding amazing things to do of astronomical proportions. It is taking the portion that we have and finding an amazing way to apply it into our everyday passage. If you are still trying to impress other people, it's because you have failed to impress yourself. If you're trying to please other people, it's because you believe you are not pleasing. If you are pushing yourself to give, it's because you're trying to impress and to please.

I am not recommending selfishness, nor am I trying to condemn those people with a generous nature. I am just explaining that poverty is an ongoing aggravation needing to be addressed with an ongoing consciousness. It is a daily problem, which demands daily attention. It is with us, so we need to find a way to address it.

Giving is a temporary situation based upon fleeting empathy. Returning is a life practice that's easy to do. Will it be enough? No. The poor will always be with us. But we should do what we can for them. And what we can do is return what we've already decided we don't really require.

It makes the closet a little barer. But after all, that just gives people an excuse to buy us more things that we can either wear or return.

If you feel the need to have two of everything, this idea will seem ridiculous. But if you're of a mind to have what you want and enjoy it, and also to follow an intelligent return policy, you've just taken another step towards living a legendary life.

-Sitting Nine-
Just Downstairs

Benny loved his mom. Of course, most kids do love their moms. But his was stronger. Benny believed he would love his mom if she weren't his mom, if you know what I mean.

She always was happy. She always seemed to have a story to go along with every problem and a joke to accompany every blessing.

They lived on the third floor in the Briargate Apartments. Benny used to complain about having to climb the stairs until his mother pointed out two very important points: *How special, she said, it is to live on the third floor! First, we get all this exercise without having to pay for a gym, and then, when we finally get to the top of the stairs, we have the most beautiful view of everything in the whole town.*

Benny had to agree, although some nights, when he was particularly tired from school, the climb did seem arduous. But always, arriving at the top, he would rejoice over seeing the vista of scenery before him.

Yeah, Mom was right.

Mom also made a point of making sure that Benny always was aware of the needs of others.

"Just downstairs," she would say. "We need to think about the folks. Maybe they don't have as much as we do. Maybe they are hurting. Maybe if we make a few extra biscuits, we could take a couple to them after dinner. Because just downstairs," she would say, "there are always people in need."

Benny wasn't sure he agreed. He knew that he and his mother were fairly poor and she had a difficult time making ends meet, although you could never tell by her disposition, nor did a word of complaint ever come off her lips.

"Just downstairs," she would say. "Those are the people in need."

So Benny visited a little girl in the apartment on the ground floor. He figured she must be really downstairs. So he toted her books, and paid for her lunch twice a week at school, and made sure that when his mother made those "extra specials" that the little girl and her family got some. The little girl was very gracious and the family was grateful for the generosity.

Benny was about eleven years old when his mother became very sick. Once again, you could hardly tell, except that she became smaller and frail and her skin turned very white. But she still continued to tell Benny "just downstairs there were people in greater need."

Benny had just turned twelve years old, springtime, when his mother passed away. He didn't have any other relatives, so the family of the little girl came to see him.

They asked him if he wanted to live with them now that his mother had passed on.

Benny said, "I don't want to be any trouble. I know that you—well—that you don't have much money."

The father, surprised, looked at Benny and then laughed. "Didn't you know? We own this apartment building. So I think we can afford one more mouth to feed."

Benny was a bit bewildered but also delighted to be part of this new family. He wondered if his mother had known that the father of this family "just downstairs" was the landlord.

He would never know. It didn't matter. The words and beauty of her philosophy live on. He never forgot what his mother said. Because no matter how low you may get in your life, there is always someone "just downstairs" from where you are.

The only way to keep gratitude fully blooming in our hearts is by returning the little bit we can to those living beneath us.

Just downstairs—another step to living a legendary life.

-Sitting Ten-
Thirty, Sixty and a Hundred

The Mandeville Marauders were a baseball team. Last season they got a new coach, Bob Stark. Coach Stark took over a team that was always playing .500 ball— won as many as they lost and lost as many as they won. Of course, no aspiring coach plans on maintaining such a record. The goal is to win more, to justify both his hiring and his techniques of motivating a team. Coach Stark had one simple rule: hit home runs.

The team practiced fielding and running, but during batting practice there would be no rehearsal of the sacrificed fly or even simulation of the bunt. Home runs. Coach Stark contended that this was the way the Marauders could be pulled out of the doldrums of a mediocre season.

There was an excitement all through spring training camp. All of the players became better at hitting the long ball and at judging pitches, waiting for the right one so they could smack it out of the park. The chatter in Mandeville was incessant. Just on the strength of word of mouth, there were more people purchasing advertisement in the program book and vendors lining up to have concession stands at the stadium. Every one was certain that Coach Stark's home run philosophy would put the Marauders in the winning column and Mandeville on the map.

The first game was against the Adamsville Athletics. The philosophy paid off. Six of the nine batters hit a home run during the game. It was so exciting—it was thrilling to see those balls flying out of the park. That's why it was perplexing when the Marauders lost the game—8 to 6. The Athletics had no home runs. But eight men had been able to cross the plate.

Coach Stark celebrated with the team the six home runs and told them, "We'll get 'em next time."

Well, next time they hit five home runs—big long ones—and lost 7 to 5 to the Terrapins. Three nights later, it was another loss, 9 to 7, to the Tigers. All in all, after six games, the Marauders players had hit thirty-four home runs, a team record, and lost all six games.

Coach Stark was at his wit's end. After the last game, a sixth loss against the Ducks, an old man emerged from the crowd and asked Coach Stark if he could have a moment of his time. He was a small fellow, the kind that would be almost invisible even in a room occupied by three people.

He sat down with the Coach and made his case. "Coach Stark, I've been watching your team for the past six games. I, myself, have never played baseball, but have always enjoyed the sport, although at times I find it a bit slow and dull."

Coach Stark frowned at the little old man, so he hurriedly continued.

"It just seems to me, Coach, that if everyone's always hitting home runs, there's no way to get anyone on base, so that when you actually do get a home run, you don't just score one person, but two, three or even four. You see, that's how they're beating you, Coach. One of their batters may strike out, followed by another one getting a base hit, and then the guy who got the base hit runs to second base, and the next guy maybe walks. Then somebody else hits a double and then the next batter hits a double, a runner scores, and then you have two runners on second and third. So your pitcher decides to walk the next batter, loading the bases. The next batter hits a fly ball, which your fielder drops, allowing two more runners to score."

Coach Stark was annoyed by the little, old man. "What is it you're trying to say, fella?" he demanded.

The old man paused for a moment and then spoke slowly. "I guess what I'm trying to say is, if everybody is trying to hit home runs, there's not enough people getting on base to make the home runs mean much."

Coach Stark piped in. "There is nothing better than a home run."

The old man paused and then replied. "Well, I think there is, sir. And that's a victory caused by the whole team working together."

As in our story, we live in a world that extols the beauty and the power of hitting the home run. Fame and fortune are portrayed as the ultimate symbols of human value. But life really doesn't work that way. Just like in baseball, life demands that we pick up the bat and take our chances. Sometimes we strike out, sometimes it's a base hit. Sometimes we walk. And sometimes we hit a double, a triple, or even a home run. The only difficulty comes when we don't recognize the value of each and every maneuver.

The Marauders found out that without base hits, home runs don't add up to victories. Without bunts and walks and stolen bases, people cannot get onto the playing field—people who add up and make a difference, and not only make the victory sweeter, but actually make the victory possible.

Sometimes opportunities come in thirties, sometimes they come in sixties and sometimes they come in hundreds. The legendary lifer knows that three thirties nearly make a hundred, and two sixties are even more.

Where are the people writing music that may never be heard by the entire world, but relished by a regional few? Where are the politicians who do not aspire to national office, but instead, make one little town a little bit of heaven? Where are the shopkeepers that will never appear on the stock exchange, but create jobs for a selected few?

Babe Ruth was arguably the greatest baseball player of all time. He was called the Home Run King. He also had the greatest ratio of strikeouts. You may feel free to aim for the fences every time you come to the plate, but if you want to live a full, legendary life, you are going to take your place on first base, and let another person hit you in. The true sense of success is in the value of the journey and the creation by our own hands of the miracle. Waiting for chance and opportunity and promotion to propel us to notoriety may create the big hit, but it rarely wins the game.

-Sitting Eleven-
UL (Unconditional Love)

Entering a diner occupied by tables and chairs with room enough when not filled by human forms, I wriggled and squirmed my way to a table and sat down for a breakfast of two eggs over easy, an order of grits overdone and a side of wheat toast over-buttered. There was a young couple sitting nearby (which, nearby could have been anywhere in the place) and they were attempting to have a private conversation, one that I tried to honor, but due to the placing of proximity, accidentally became a party to.

Boy: You know I love you.

Girl: But what kind of love?

Boy: What do you mean, what kind of love?

Girl: Well, there is *eros* and *phila* and then there's *agape*.

Boy: (giggling) You just made those up, didn't you?

Girl: This isn't funny.

Me: Slurp, slurp, cough, cough, throat clear, throat clear. (I was trying to let them know that I could overhear their conversation but they were rather involved.)

Boy: I wasn't laughing at you.

Girl: No, you were laughing at love.

Me: (Internal groan)

Boy: I wasn't laughing at love.

Girl: Yes, you were.

Boy: No, I wasn't.

Girl: Yes, you were.

(This went on a little bit longer, but for brevity's sake and to honor the wise use of paper, I will shorten it for your convenience.)

Boy: What do you want me to say?

Girl: I want you to say you love me with *agape* love—that's His love.

Boy: Not to be disrespectful, hon, but I think we do some things that He...wouldn't, if you know what I mean.

Girl: I mean inside.

Boy: Okay. Go on.

Girl: I have always dreamed of someone loving me with unconditional love—like He loves me.

Boy: I do.

Girl: You don't.

Boy: I do.

Girl: You don't.

(Same situation, and brevity, etc...)

Boy: So how would you know that I loved you with unconditional love?

Girl: I just would.

Boy: Could you be a bit more specific?

Girl: Well...you would love me just the way I am and wouldn't want to change me.

Boy: And that's His love?

Girl: Yes. That's the Father's love. *Agape.*

Boy: So, you're saying that God doesn't want to change us?

Girl: Yes. He loves us just the way we are.

Boy: So why does He ask us to repent?

Girl: Are you arguing with me?

Boy: No. Just curious.

Girl: Now what was your question again?

Boy: I mean, why does He want us to become different if we're okay the way we are?

Girl: Well, that's easy. It's for our own good.

Boy: Well, you know I would never argue with you, but whether it's for our own good or not, He's still saying that He wants us different, right?

Girl: Yes. But He loves us even if we aren't different. See what I mean?

Boy: So you're saying if we don't change, and don't become what He suggests we become, we're still okay?

Girl: You're confusing me.

Boy: I don't want to do that. I just want to make sure I get this right, because, like, honestly, I don't want to talk about it again, if you know what I mean.

Girl: No.

Boy: I said that poorly. What I'm trying to say is, if God makes suggestions to us, like in the Bible, and we don't follow them, like, will we still go to heaven?

Girl: No—to go to heaven you have to be born again.

Boy: So aren't we being forced to say, "I really screwed up being born the first time?"

Girl: No. It's saying that there is a gift from God that is available to you to make your life better.

Boy: Once again—not trying to make trouble. But if it's a gift, and I decide I don't want it, or even if I turn it down and say I'm happy where I am, does that mean that He will still, like, let me go to heaven?

Girl: Probably not.

Boy: So if I don't go to heaven, what's that leave?

Girl: Let's not talk about that. That's bad.

Boy: Once again, I'm trying to understand. What I'm trying to ask...

Girl: (interrupting) Okay. You'll go to hell. Is that what you wanted to hear?

Boy: Not particularly. That's my point. You say that God loves me without condition...

Girl: He does. The way I want to be loved.

Boy: But if I don't do what He suggests, even though it's a really good gift, don't get me wrong, but if I decide, like, to pass on it, then, what you're saying is, He expresses his unconditional love by sending me to hell...

Girl: God doesn't send anyone to hell. We choose to go there...

Boy: I don't think so. Sounds like, pretty much, we get sent there...

Girl: You just don't understand spiritual matters. Which is why you don't understand me. Which is why...I don't know...maybe we can just never be happy together...

Boy: Understand, I'm workin' here...tryin' to get it down. So you say you unconditionally love me...

Girl: I do.

90

Boy: (continuing) On the condition that I can unconditionally love you and accept everything about you even if something you're doing is not the best thing for you, right?

Girl: You are really confused.

Boy: (under his breath) One of us...

Girl: Pardon?

Boy: I just don't think there's any such thing as unconditional love. I think if you love someone, you're going to tell them if you think something stupid is going on, or if they're hurting themselves, or if you just don't understand something they're doing because it bugs you...

Girl: If you love someone, it shouldn't bug you.

Boy: Everybody bugs everybody, right? It doesn't mean we don't love each other...It just means, well, it means we're bugable, I guess.

Girl: All I know is I need unconditional love. *Agape.*

Boy: Well, I can give you God's love, if that's what you mean.

Girl: That's all I can ask.

Me: (I was hoping at this point that the young man would leave it at that, but there seems to be something inside the male of our species that is determined to always discover the tiny wrinkle in the rug to trip over)

Boy: Okay. I'll give you God's love. If you don't repent and do what I say, I'll make your life hell. (He laughed)

I quickly grabbed my check and ran to the cash register to avoid the female explosion that I knew was about to occur. I paid my bill and exited the establishment, taking one final glance through the window at the feuding pair. She sat with her arms folded across her chest with a little pucker on her lips while he continued to talk, rather, apologize and explain, with vivid gestures and frantic hand movements.

I thought to myself, how ludicrous it was for us to believe that anything in life is unconditional! Even the unconditional guarantee on my electric razor is followed by two paragraphs of tiny print telling me how it can be revoked. Am I to become cynical over this or merely practical?

Honestly, I don't want your unconditional love. I want you to tell me when I really look bad in that pair of shorts. I want you to tell me if you're concerned about my health. I want you to disagree with me when you think I'm dumb and I want you to give me the right to do the same with you. Surely I want you to rejoice with me when I rejoice and join me in my lamentations, but I also need you to tell me when I become too silly or I'm feeling sorry for myself. Of course, you could be wrong. But I still need to hear the disagreeable voice to keep me balanced and on the straight and narrow of self-awareness.

And by the way, Larry, I'd like you to do the same for me. Unconditional love is reserved for silly adolescents and greeting card companies. Legendary people know that conditions on love are often the best way of expressing the emotion.

-Sitting Twelve-
The Clay Way

Henry Clay was known as the "Great Compromiser." Although he ran for President of the United States five times and lost, the main thrust of his political career was in Congress, negotiating the particular "deal of the day." Although the Washingtons and Lincolns are extolled by the history books as great leaders, Henry Clay is rarely mentioned in the same breath. It certainly isn't because of inactivity. He was probably the most powerful political figure of his era. It's because he was the great compromiser. And, in fulfilling this mission, he ended up negotiating matters that really should never have been negotiated. For you see, Henry Clay found himself in the position of trying to compromise a deal between the North and South and the emerging states of the Union over the issue of slavery. Although most historians will agree that Henry Clay, himself, was opposed to the institution, he felt it was more important to maintain the status quo of a peaceful union than to pursue the excellence of a slave-free society.

When is it right to be peaceful? And when is it necessary to raise the fuss that creates the change that fosters new attitudes that lead to a better world? There is the question. There are just some things that will be compromised and some things that are not negotiable.

In leading a legendary life, perhaps the greatest attribute to attain is *discernment*. And specifically, discerning what is changing, what needs to change, what will change and what must remain the same. If you mix these up, you end up on the short end of the stick, with history viewing you as an encumbrance. So how do we know the difference? How do we determine what is flowing toward evolution and what is carved into the face of the mountain?

I'm taking a moment in this chapter to divide these into three distinct categories.

Number 1: Spiritual Truth.

Number 2: Moral Values

Number 3: Social Standards.

Almost everything I can think of that comes up in our everyday lives falls into one of these three categories. I'm sure it could be divided into many more segments, but for a working dialogue, let us begin here. I will tell you right now that it is impossible to lead a legendary life and be of use to your fellow man if you hold absolutes in all three of these categories.

I remember as a boy, various demons would rise up in society about every five years. First came communism. Then a variation—socialism. And then, it was something as trivial as long hair, and then it became issues of war followed by a reevaluating of our sexual mores, materialism, greed, homosexuality, religiosity and terrorism. Each one of these, and perhaps many other sub-topics, rose to the forefront as the most frightening, debilitating and incriminating challenge of the time.

But as it turned out, McCarthy wasn't right about communism. Actually, communism was its own worst enemy. Long hair didn't make boys turn into girls and radicals but instead was just, well, was just long hair. The domino theory of communism taking over the entire continent of Asia didn't happen and the 55,000 young men and women who died in Vietnam did so in an unfulfilled mission.

In each case, the controversies raised were an attempt to maintain the traditions of our times without giving in to the pressure of pounding change. They left us holding an unholy bag of excuses, scrambling for higher ground to justify our former positions.

There were things I was taught as a child in our religiously based society that have changed and have morphed into new beliefs in our present structure.

For instance, as a boy I was taught that divorce was a sin and evil in God's eyes. Now, is there a church in America that doesn't offer seminars on surviving divorce, or even a dating service for those who have lost their first partners?

A tremor of trauma trembled through the ecclesiastical world at the notion of guitars and drums and any predilection for retiring the old hymns in favor of newer writings. Move ahead a decade. Is there a church anywhere now that doesn't offer some sort of modern service with contemporary music, complemented by some once-thought unholy combo of instruments?

It is impossible to live a legendary life without being aware of what is truly important as opposed to what is naturally transient. Let us begin with a bold statement. No spiritual truth is an absolute. Why? Because none of us are spiritual. We are all emotionally based creatures with strong physical yearnings, great mental capacity that is tainted by our fluctuating moods and a spiritual side that often struggles for space, if not air to breathe. You can spend your life trying to reject your own personal nature. You can deny yourself to the point of abuse, but it will not change the fact that we are temporary beings trying to understand eternal matters.

THERE IS NOTHING WRONG WITH THE GREAT DISCUSSION. What is the great discussion? Who are we, why are we, where did we come from and where in the hell are we going? Feel free to participate with gusto at will. Just do not be so arrogant or ignorant to build a fort in any particular idea. Larry is an ongoing process. People who think they know his address, telephone number and all of his personal habits are not only laughable, but potentially dangerous.

I heard a preacher the other day on television quote the great Hebrews scripture, "Jesus is the same yesterday, today and forever." I had to smile. For most assuredly, the minister's interpretation was that what Moses believed about God is still true today. When actually, that scripture means that Jesus, who was in a constant state of learning and growing in stature and wisdom while he was mortal on this planet, was always that way and is still learning and growing and expanding today. I cannot believe in a deity that asks me to repent at whim while maintaining a permanent residence with no revision.

It isn't that I'm trying to change what Larry is thinking or what Larry even may will. It's just that I'm sometimes dumb—but still smart enough to know that the matters of universal truth should not be placed in my care and safekeeping.

Spiritual absolutes, in one way or another, are the source of all conflict, all wars and all abusive treatment, human-to-human and even creature-to-creature.

So what should be our approach with matters of the spirit? Should spiritual decisions be determined in the court of moral judgment?

When I was a boy, I was told that it was not good that the races mix, and God forbid if black and white should ever marry.

I was provided with a basketful of reasons for this, usually culminating with, "It's just not good for the kids." It was presented to me as a moral issue. In other words, interracial dating and marriage was an immoral practice, similar to the iniquity of divorce. And then, people who determine the moral temperature of our times fell in love with people of other races and sometimes divorced their mates. So gradually, almost undetectable by the naked eye, the moral climate of our country changed. Blacks were no longer subordinate. It was considered to be passé to think such a thing. Divorce was not a sin any more, it was a mistake, in some cases just a natural evolution in the search for our soul mate.

And here I was, left holding the bag containing all of these outdated philosophies and pamphlets on moral absolutes. Being the inquisitive sort, I questioned why these ideas were even promoted in the first place. After much throat clearing and hemming and hawing, I was given a rather lengthy explanation of what they had really intended. Bewildered, I marched on to see more casualties amongst the ranks of things deemed morally absolute. For you see, those who determine such matters found it impossible to live up to their own moral codes. That's the problem with trying to be superior. What you end up creating is a moral Frankenstein that lumbers along, eventually killing off the very people you hoped to benefit. We were not meant to totally understand Larry and certainly not to become him.

For a certain season, there may actually be a majority of people who feel a particular way on some moral issue. But time, discovery, humanity and weakness soon riddle the ranks of that army of the resolute, leaving us with only a small platoon of believers.

Yes, we are just too human to be sure about anything morally.

So honestly, as livers of legendary lives, we dare not lock and load on issues of spirituality or moral correctness. It's changing, folks. If you fight it, it will fight back, and it will win. So what are the absolutes in life? What are the things that are immutable? Do they actually exist? Is there a compass, or is life just a boat without a rudder and an oar?

I believe there are only three absolutes in this life from which we draw all the energy for decision-making and interaction with our human fellows.

1. There are no chosen people. Just folks who choose to stay involved. Every time we have tried to isolate one group of people off for exemplary behavior or as a superior race, we have used both spiritual and moral constrictions to prove our contention and the end result has always been destructive. We are not chosen. We are here. And if that is not enough, then any attempt to improve our status by birth, doctrine, proclamation, skin color, national origin or sexual preference is a futile adventure in fatalism.

If you must think you're special, be prepared to always be trumped by those with a stronger case and more militant inclinations.

2. Any belief in a supreme being that doesn't place human beings in a primal role is erred. I can just hear the groans and the moans from the religiously fervent from all over the world. "He's trying to make people God." No. I'm just trying to say that it's impossible to reach Larry without respecting and giving place to Bob and Sally. I never found Larry to be a judge, but he is fastidious and anal in his evaluation of how we treat one another.

There is only one absolute that comes to play in blending the supernatural and the natural. It's phrased in many different ways but the end conclusion is the same. We must duplicate in other people what we want done for ourselves. Yes, what goes around comes around. There is no value in believing in a supreme existence without celebration and reverence over the present existence. Any breach in this practice, or any attempt to circumvent human beings and their needs and value in a quest to gain favor with an eternal creature is not only fruitless, but the source for any damnation that might transpire.

3. We are evolving towards simplicity. The only thing that is certain on this planet is that things will change and ultimately, that change is an evolution toward simplicity. If you want to get into the flow of the cosmos, as it were, find a simpler path and a plainer, more direct way of dealing with others and the everyday things that make life tick.

Complexity is what invites dogma.

Complexity is what creates inst-itutions of higher confusion. Complexity is what teases us into believing we are deep.

Complexity is what causes the philosopher to ruminate over things that don't really matter, the theologian to preach homilies that homogenize nothing, and the politician to pass laws that make the inevitable illegal. Keep it simple, stupid.

There you go. Now, there is a saying you could place on a monument and mount in every courtyard in America that could be an ultimate truth that would never change through the centuries and the millennia to come. In a thousand years, someone would walk by that monument and read: "Keep it simple, stupid" and have to shake their head and go, "Right on, man."

These three social absolutes bring balance to the spiritual, tenderness to the moral and integrity to the masses. To lead a legendary life is to allow the spiritually inflexible to evolve and the morally judgmental to falter in their own hypocrisy while simply accepting the joy of:

There are no chosen people.

Human beings are to play a primal role.

And, when all is said and done, **it is the simple path that leads to Larry.**

So. You can either follow the example of the Great Compromiser, Henry Clay, and end up negotiating the destiny of men already deemed equal in a higher court of understanding, or you can abandon the foolishness of spiritual and moral absolutes and deal with the round, rotating world. After all, it's the only one we know for sure that exists.

-Sitting Thirteen-
Legendary Clifford

Candidly, I don't know why every book doesn't do it. It seems like a very smart move—we live in a time when people are busy (or at least perceive themselves to be) and they want everything condensed, micro waved, abbreviated, abridged, shortened and trimmed. Therefore many people, rather than reading a whole book, will purchase what they call the Cliff Notes. So at this point in my little presentation, I would like to create my own Cliff Notes, which I have dubbed "The Legendary Clifford" (partially because I thought Clifford sounded a bit more high-class, and also to avoid any lawsuits from the Cliff Notes folks.)

Facts are that if you have gotten this far in my book, you are a determined reader and it is my sincere hope that you have enjoyed yourself. But if, in the future, you would like to refer back and don't necessarily have time to read the whole volume, please remember to turn to lucky Sitting 13—the Clifford Notes on Living a Legendary Life, and feel free to peruse to what I hope will be your heart's content.

In Sitting One we discover that Larry sees. It is important to know that we are not alone, and that our efforts, whether miniscule or immense, are being viewed and appreciated by a force beyond ourselves. So with that in mind, slow your life down a little bit, stop multi-tasking, notice the subtle changes that occur around you, especially in yourself, and acknowledge that there are other people who are pursuing excellence and are fully aware of Larry and his viewing.

Cruising into Sitting Two, we discussed the notion that *You Never Really Get What You Need* and that actually, lack begets lack. We finish the sitting off with the realization that you sometimes get what you want, and facts are, you always get what's next.

Now in Sitting Three, we introduced *ISA*—a trio of troublers to the human condition, that when added to the normal circumstances of life, create all the difficulties that plague us. That trio was *insecurity* and *superstition,* culminating in *arrogance.* But we also discussed the fact that life counteracts these troublers with a triumphant three—*acceptance, logic* and *humility.*

The horror of *Babble-On*, Sitting Four, was a commentary on the incessant need in our society to be appreciated. Living a legendary life is rejecting false acclaim in favor of lasting satisfaction.

The Art of Flaunting, a little passage we dubbed Sitting Five, was a fun journey in discovering how powerful it can be to be wrong if admitting it at the precise moment of the commission is achieved. Yes, truly—flaunt your mistakes and join the human race.

One of the more lengthy sittings in the book is entitled *From Whence*. There are five notorious dripping faucets that dribble all of the compounds for failure. They are *anticipation, confusion, conviction, positive thinking* and *hope*. Life grants us a wonderful balance by offering us an additional five that foster the compounds for success: *questioning, humor, reasoning, distraction* and *relinquishment*.

Lucky Sitting Seven was the *Danger of PONDering*. Together we learned that there's nothing wrong with being a big fish in a little pond. Living a legendary life is facing reality without opinion. What if our life ends up being exactly what it is? Would we be disappointed? Or would we find that we had fodder enough to feed our human frenzy?

Sitting Eight—*It's Not Really Giving.* It is returning. Returning back to life that portion we did not need or did not use, and doing it quickly to keep the cycle of flow going amongst our fellow man. Obviously, that means things will trickle down our way, too.

We told a little story in Sitting Nine, entitled *Just Downstairs.* One of the main problems we have in our society is that everyone thinks they are a little poor—so no one is willing to become the benefactor. No matter what financial or social standing we may be in, each of us can enrich others because there is always someone who lives "just downstairs" from our perch.

Thirty, Sixty and a Hundred—Sitting Ten, was a discovery of how nothing is really lost. Although our efforts are often absorbed into a greater conclusion, the fact of the matter is, hitting home runs does not win games unless there are people already on base.

It was a little dialogue between a boy and a girl in Sitting Eleven that created the climate for a discussion on *UL (Unconditional Love.)* Conditions on love are often the best way of expressing that emotion.

And finally, in Sitting Twelve, we were introduced to *The Clay Way*. Henry Clay, the Great Compromiser, who wielded tremendous political power in his day, had five failed attempts at running for President and basically, has disappeared into obscurity—at least, in the flow of common knowledge. We closed the sitting by saying that there are no spiritual or moral absolutes. It's not that "situation ethics" rules supreme, just really that there are three statements that are unchangeable. *1) There are no chosen people, just people who choose to stay involved; 2) every belief in a supreme being that does not put humans in a primal role is erred; 3) we are ever evolving towards greater simplicity.*

Well there you have it—a brief, concise summary of **Living a Legendary Life**—my Clifford Notes, if you will.

I hope you enjoyed the book and I hope you will read it again. But when you want to remember one of those specific things, or just a general overlook, feel free to flip to Thirteen and rediscover or share at will.

-Sitting Fourteen-
The Announcement

Larry is missing.

No one is quite sure when it happened, so therefore, how it occurred remains a mystery also. Upon investigation, it was discovered that everything is in place. All his duties are still being performed. He just seems, well, as I said, missing.

Some doomsayers have begun to proclaim that he's dead, but they are the same ones that really never appreciated him in the first place, some totally ignoring his existence. Vigils have begun. Search parties have been organized and clues collected. A series of depositions have been taken from possible contacts. There have also been some rather dubious tactics by vigilante groups, which have gathered up suspects who they believe may be involved in foul play.

But Larry is missing. Some people don't seem that concerned about it, never having actually known Larry that well, or finding him distant and foreboding. But for whatever reason, Larry seems to have vanished. He has done this before. Larry is an independent sort who tends to favor those who share his profile. But it seems—well, it seems a little longer this time.

Some people say he's going to come back—real soon. Other people have made paintings and images of him, trying to remember a smile here, a flick of an eye there, a particular brow furrow. But it isn't the same.

Larry just sometimes likes to go away, like into a far country. Then he will come back and act as if nothing has ever happened, expecting us to continue on as if he were here, even demanding an inventory of our activities. Some people find this behavior bizarre and annoying. Other people invent new Larrys to replace the out-of-pocket eternal one. (I've even heard a rumor that he was in Stockholm for sexual reassignment. Wouldn't that be a kick in the pants if Larry came back as Lauren? I wonder if that would bother me, if Lauren were watching me? I guess I'd be fine except during shower time.)

Well, wherever he or she is, with whomever, right now he/she seems missing.

It's really quite interesting how dependent people become upon Larry's presence. I mean, it isn't like the words and philosophies and attitudes are absent from us. They are still here, available, functioning and transforming. It's just that some people feel the need to fill some sort of "Larry space." Maybe that's why he goes missing.

Or maybe terrorists kidnapped him. They may have taken him away and blindfolded him so he can't see anymore—thrust into some old shed on the south side of an oil field.

Wow.

Makes for quite a story, doesn't it? People love stories. Sometimes people love stories better than reality. I guess that's all right, as long as truth isn't lost in the tale.

What's that, you ask? What do I plan on doing?

Well, I don't see any reason to stop doing what I always did. 'Cause facts are, although we hope for a heaven, we are only guaranteed an earth. And while we dream of eternity, we live in the moment. So I guess my plan is to keep doing what I've learned. And keep believing that Larry, wherever he may be, is still watching. Because whether he is or not, my life is enriched in knowing.

So here's to Larry. May he enjoy his vacation. I think he's earned one. And in his absence, which I assume will be temporary, here's to you and me—the best

112

evidence to the fact that he existed in the first place.

And here's to living a legendary life.

The End.

Jonathan Richard Cring

Jonathan Richard Cring is the composer of fourteen symphonies, the author of eleven books, including **I'M . . . the legend of the son of man, Liary, Holy Peace . . .the story of Iz and Pal, Jesonian, Finding the Lily, Digging for Gold and 20 other reasons to kiss a frog.** His thirty-year experience has taken him from the grease paint of theater to a time as an evangelist among the gospel saints. He is the winner of a Billboard Music Award and is the in-house composer for the Sumner County Symphony. He travels the country lecturing as an advocate for the Jesonian movement. He has been married for thirty-five years and is the father of three sons and guardian to three others. He lives in Hendersonville, Tennessee.

Also from the Author

All books available through Amazon.com and
WWW.LWSBOOKS.COM

20 other reasons to kiss a frog
ISBN 978-0-9704361-4-6

Leaping into the mainstream of social consciousness and
human interactions, Jonathan Richard Cring offers his new non-
fiction volume 20 OTHER REASONS TO KISS A FROG, a look
at today's life with parallels and insight from our friend in the
pond. Featuring titles like: THEY TREAT ALL WOMEN LIKE
PRINCESSES, THEY KEEP THEIR TONGUES TO
THEMSELVES and THEY ARE NOT ASHAMED OF THEIR
TADPOLE YEARS the fast-paced sittings offer comedy and
insight--a human blending of delight.

Jesonian
A decision to take spirituality personally.
ISBN 978-0-9704361-4-6

Stagnancy is the decision to settle for less than we know we need.
In every generation there must be a voice reminding us of our true
mission, prodding us on to escape mediocrity and stirring the waters
to freshen the stream of thinking. Jesonian is a book that poses the

Also from Jonathan Richard Cring

questions in the heart of every human who seeks to find some nourishment for his hardening soul – every man, woman and child who yearns for a message with meaning and wants to escape the rigors of religion and find the true spirit in spirituality.

Finding the Lily (to consider)
A journette of the journey.
ISBN 978-0-9704361-5-3

When I was a kid, they didn't have Big Men's Stores - at least, none my parents told me about. So my mother would buy me the only pants she could find in my size - work pants.

Dickie work pants. For some reason, she would choose the green ones - the color created by smashing a bag of green peas into a frog. And speaking of being smashed, for some reason, she wouldn't buy them my size, I guess because she didn't want to admit how big I was. And so she would purchase them so small that I would have to suck in to button them. That's what you like when you're fat. Tight green clothes. Of course, these pants were so stiff they could stand by themselves, which I have to admit, came in handy when waiting in line at an amusement park.

Digging for Gold *[in the rule]*
ISBN 978-0-9704361-6-0

The Golden Rule, Do unto others as you would have them do unto you, loses some of its gleam and luster when merely decoupaged and hung on a wall in a Sunday School class as some sort of insipid platitude, more an aspiration than a lifestyle.

In DIGGING FOR GOLD (in the rule), author Cring examines the intricacies and passion of the original thought and also offers innovative approaches to turning the "Rule" into a reality.

Chocked full of stories, examples and plans of action, DIGGING is a must for the soul who desires to have their spirituality flowing in the mainstream instead of entombed in the sanctuary of religious redundancy.

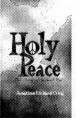

Holy Peace . . . the story of Iz and Pal
ISBN 978-0-9704361-3-9

In a basket full of oranges, it is always the singular apple that gains our attention. This is a wonderful characteristic of the human soul. So in our day and age, in the midst of clamoring for resolutions based on military might, a breath of fresh air comes in to the atmosphere of pending war. Amir and Jubal – two boys who grew up on different sides of the tracks of a conflict – one Arab, one Jew. They rename themselves Iz and Pal and determine to maintain their

friendship amidst the granite – headed thinking of their
friendship amidst the granite-headed thinking of their society.
Where their journey takes them, the friends they make along
the way, the surprising enemies, and the stunning resolution,
will keep you riveted to the brief pages of this odyssey into
peace.

I'M ...
the legend of the son of man
ISBN 978-0-9704361-3-9

A novel on the life of Jesus Christ focusing on his
humanity, passion, and personality—highlighting
struggles with his family, sexuality, abduction by zealots,
humor and wit, and interaction with characters bound by
tradition, affection, legalism, politics, and religious
fanaticism—congealed into a 416 page entertaining and
inspirational quick read; non-theological and mind
enriching.

Preparing a Place *[for myself]*
ISBN 978-0-9704361-7-7

The perfect book for all those folks who would like to die just long enough to find out what the crap is going on – then come back to pizza. I always wanted to meet God. When I was a child, very small, I thought he would look like Reverend Bacorra, a Presbyterian minister I knew- salt and pepper hair, tall, glasses, donning a black robe, wearing oxblood, shiny shoes with scuffed tips.

As I grew older my image changed, but always, I envisioned a physical presence – an actual being. Now, where was God?

I wondered if God was merely light, love and spirit. I smiled at my own ramblings. Light, love and spirit - not a bad triangle.

Still, I wanted to meet God, fact to face, as it were.
a bad triangle.
Still, I wanted to meet God, fact to face, as it were.

Also from Jonathan Richard Cring

Mr. Kringle's Tales . . . 26 stories 'til Christmas
ISBN 978-0-9704361-1-5
Twenty-six great Christmas stories for young and old An advent calendar of stories ranging from the hilarious "Gunfight at the Okay Chorale" to the spine-chilling "Mr. Kringle Visits the President", to the futuristic "Daviatha".

Ask for these titles at all titles from
LWS Books at:

• Your local bookstore
• www.lwsbooks.com
• www.amazon.com

Printed in the United States
54021LVS00003B/1-240